P9-EKD-854

Exciting Origami

Origami Arts and Crafts

EMANUELE AZZITÀ

Enslow Publishing
101 W. 23rd Street
Suite 240
New York, NY 10011
USA
enslow.com

This edition published in 2018 by Enslow Publishing, LLC.
101 W. 23rd Street, Suite 240, New York, NY 10011

Library of Congress Cataloging-in-Publication Data

Names: Azzitá, Emanuele, author.
Title: Origami arts and crafts / Emanuele Azzitá.
Description: New York, NY : Enslow Publishing, 2018. | Series: Exciting origami |
   Includes bibliographical references and index. | Audience: 3-6.
Identifiers: LCCN 2017005207| ISBN 9780766086463 (library bound) | ISBN
   9780766087613 (paperback) | ISBN 9780766087620 (6 pack)
Subjects: LCSH: Origami—Juvenile literature.
Classification: LCC TT872.5 .A985 2018 | DDC 736/.982—dc23
LC record available at https://lccn.loc.gov/2017005207

Printed in the United States of America

To Our Readers: We have done our best to make sure all websites in this book were active and appropriate when we went to press. However, the author and the publisher have no control over and assume no liability for the material available on those websites or on any websites they may link to. Any comments or suggestions can be sent by e-mail to customerservice@enslow.com.

All images © by DVE Publishing, worldwide, branch of Confidential Concepts, USA except cover background pattern, Tarapong Siri/Shutterstock.com and confetti Vjom/Shutterstock.com.

CONTENTS

INTRODUCTION

Origami is, simply put, the art of creating figures (people, animals, flowers, and more) using just a piece of paper. Fantasy and creativity are the key elements in origami design: prove your skills, unleash your imagination, and discover the excitement and fun of creating your own crafts out of paper. You can embark on this adventure alone or with your friends, and you only need two things: joy and creativity!

In the following pages you'll find plenty of ideas to create plants and decorations (frames, bracelets, tulips, and more) for your bedroom, classroom, or even as a present for someone special. The beginning, of course, won't be easy—that's why you should start with the simplest projects. But with a little bit of practice you'll be able to create new, unique decorations, turning simple sheets of paper into original objects. This is a great challenge for you and your friends. Good luck...and may the best origami artist win!

MATERIALS

Origami is a great hobby you can practice anytime and with only a few materials: you just need a sheet of paper, a book, and someplace to work. Of course, you should pay attention to the quality of the paper. To make beautiful, long-lasting objects, use paper appropriate for your goal. We recommend sheets of paper that:

- Are not too rigid, since you'll have a hard time folding them.
- Are not too thin, since they will tear easily.
- Are resistant and somewhat rigid, so you can create easy crease patterns.

You can find high-quality paper specifically designed for origami, but you don't need this paper when you're just beginning. At first, try using:

- Magazine paper. The pages will be full of colorful photos, adding an original and elegant touch to your creations.
- Construction paper.
- Metallic foil paper. This paper will give you an easy way to outline the edges of your figures.
- Wrapping paper.

To make your creations, you need to fold the sheets carefully. If you need to, feel free to use your nails to go over each crease. This will make it easier to create lasting, defined folds. Even though scissors aren't used in traditional origami, they might be useful for some figures. Go ahead and use them if you want—don't worry about it!

FRAME

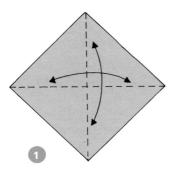

1

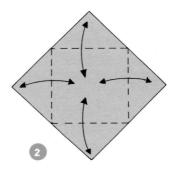

2

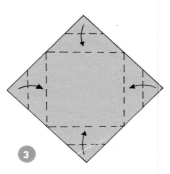

3

1-2 Fold along the lines and unfold.

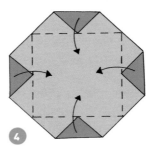

4

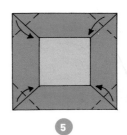

5

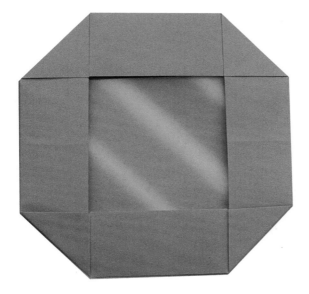

3 Fold the tips of each corner along the crease pattern you made.

4-5 Fold along the lines.

6

BRACELET

1 Fold along the lines and unfold.

2-4 Fold along the lines to make a thin, vertical crease pattern.

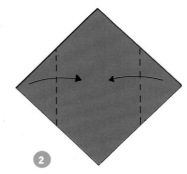

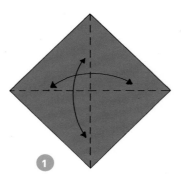

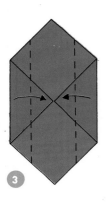

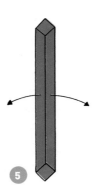

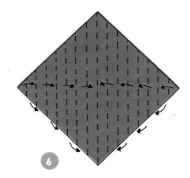

5 Unfold entirely.

6 Create an accordion fold along the crease pattern from each end, meeting in the middle.

7 Join the two ends together.

SAILBOAT

1 Fold along the line and unfold.

2-3 Fold along the line.

4-6 Fold along the lines.

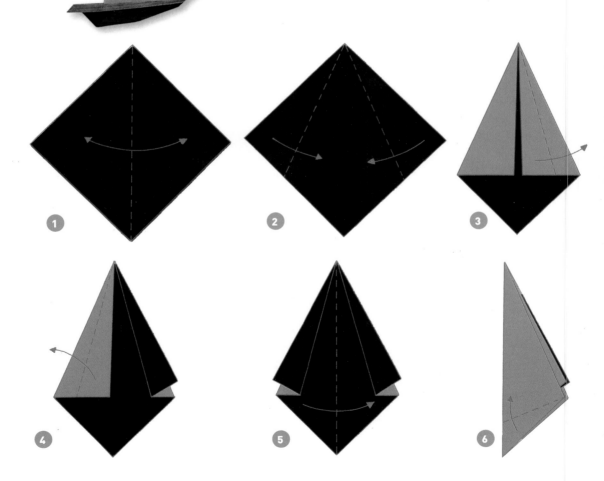

7   Fold the flap backwards along the line.

8   Unfold.

9   Push the flap out and over the bottom corner.

10-12   Fold along the line in both directions.

13   Fold down the edge of the boat.

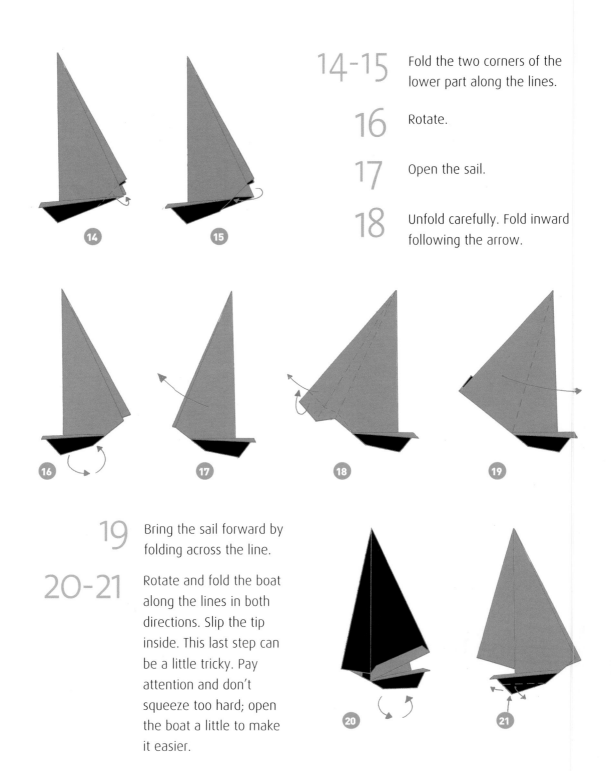

14-15 Fold the two corners of the lower part along the lines.

16 Rotate.

17 Open the sail.

18 Unfold carefully. Fold inward following the arrow.

19 Bring the sail forward by folding across the line.

20-21 Rotate and fold the boat along the lines in both directions. Slip the tip inside. This last step can be a little tricky. Pay attention and don't squeeze too hard; open the boat a little to make it easier.

TENT

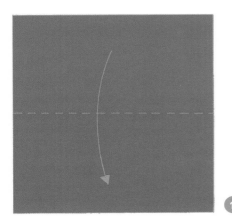

1-2   Fold along the lines.

3-4   Lift and turn out.

5   Rotate and repeat this step on the other side.

6   Fold along the lines, creating a waterbomb base.

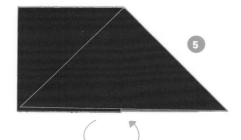

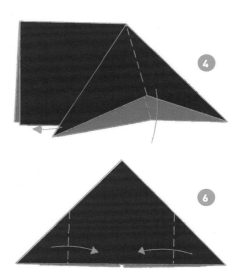

7 Fold along the lines and open again.

8 Lift the central part to make it coincide with the top point by bringing the two side corners together.

9 Fold backward along the lines.

10 Lift the flaps by folding the inner corners partway along the lines.

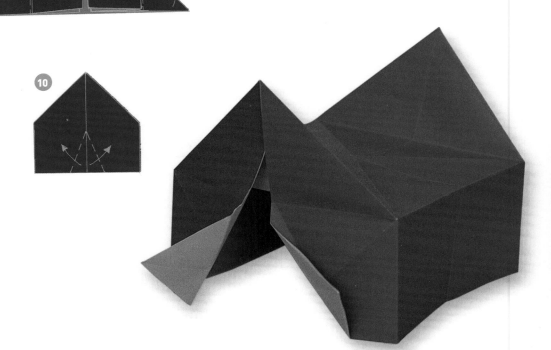

MUShROOM

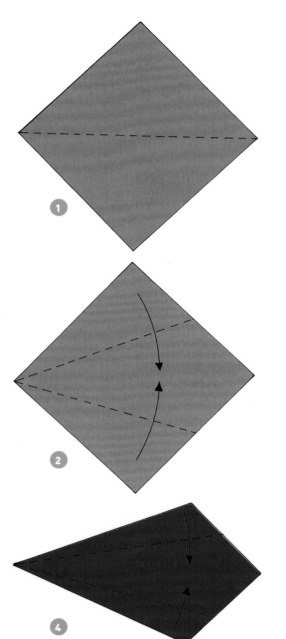

1 Fold along the line and unfold.

2 Fold along the lines.

3 Rotate.

4-5 Fold along the lines and bring the two inner corners together.

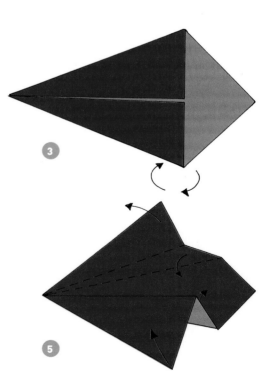

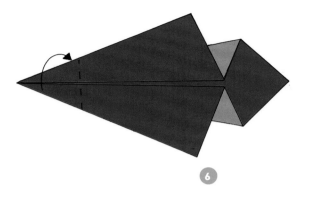

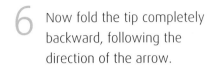
6 Now fold the tip completely backward, following the direction of the arrow.

7 Fold backward along the line.

8 Fold in both directions.

9 Push the tip down between the flaps.

10-11 Squash fold both corners inside the flaps to match the picture.

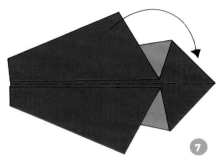

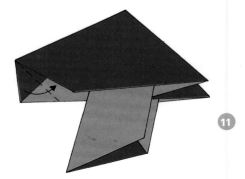

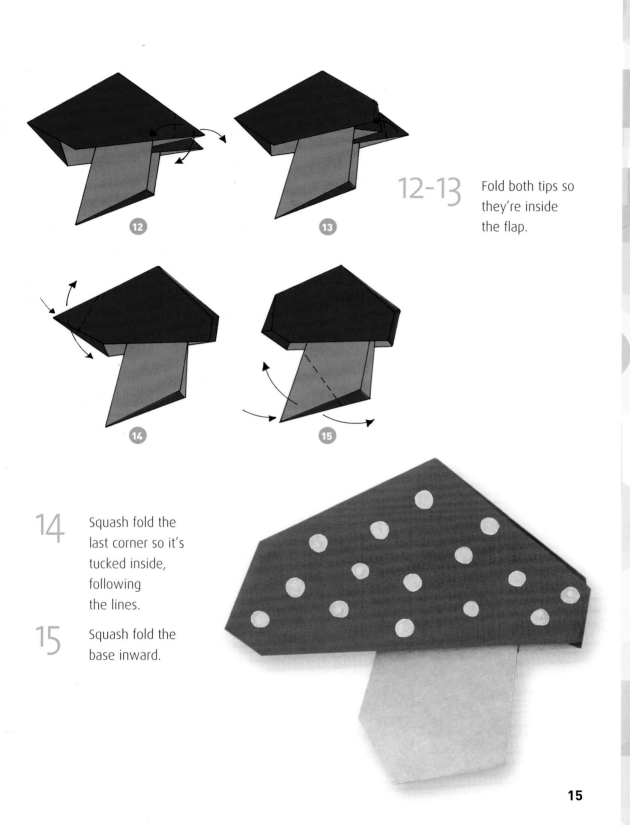

12-13 Fold both tips so they're inside the flap.

14 Squash fold the last corner so it's tucked inside, following the lines.

15 Squash fold the base inward.

BAMBOO STALK

1 Fold an A4 sheet of paper along the lines and unfold.

2 Fold along the lines, following the arrows.

3 Fold along the lines.

4 Fold along the lines.

5 Open again.

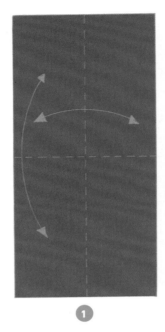

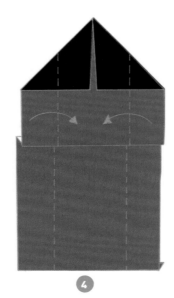

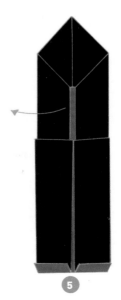

6 Fold and lift the upper part, following the arrow.

7 Fold along the line and slip the right edge into the left pocket.

8 Roll the sheet into a tube.

9 Now you have the stalk.

10-12 To make the leaf, fold a square sheet along the lines.

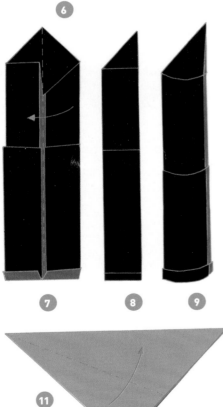

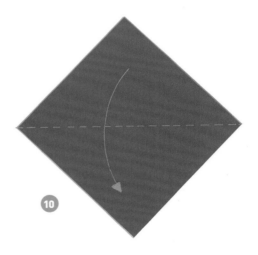

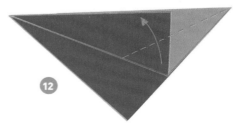

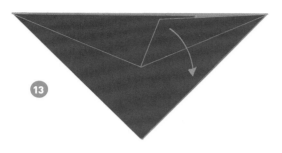

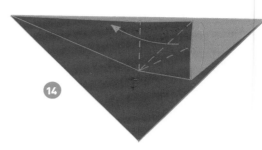

13   Open the flap.

14   Fold, following the arrows.

15   Fold along the lines until you've reached the design shown.

16   Fold along the lines and bring the tip down.

17   Fold the flaps backward.

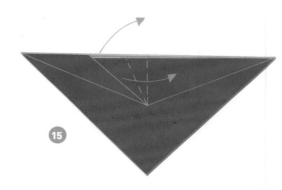

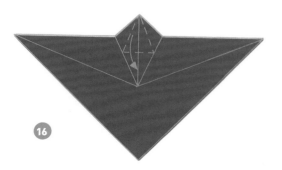

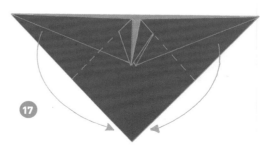

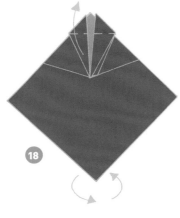

18 Fold along the line and lift the tip. Rotate.

19 Fold in both directions.

20 Lift both flaps by folding along the line and create squash folds along the vertical axis.

21 Put the flaps down again.

22 Fold in half along the vertical axis.

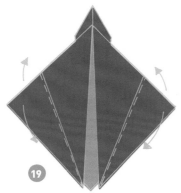

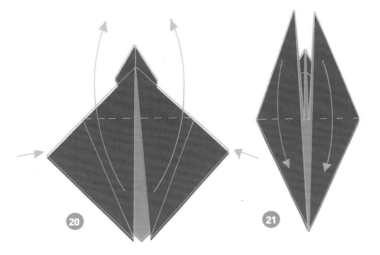

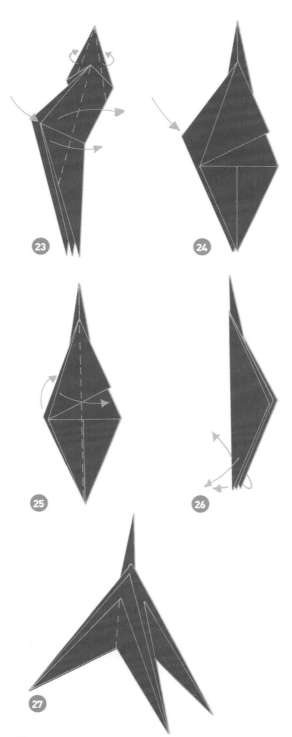

23 Fold along the line, following the arrows. Squeeze the tip to flatten it.

24 Once you're done with the last step, repeat it on the opposite side.

25 Fold the two flaps along the lines, following the arrows.

26 Separate the tips slowly, a little at a time.

27 Arrange it how you like.

28 Now you have the leaf!

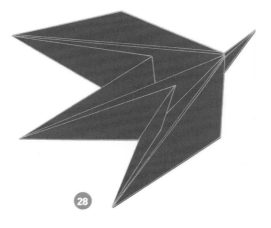

29 Slip the upper flap inside the crease of the stalk that you've already made.

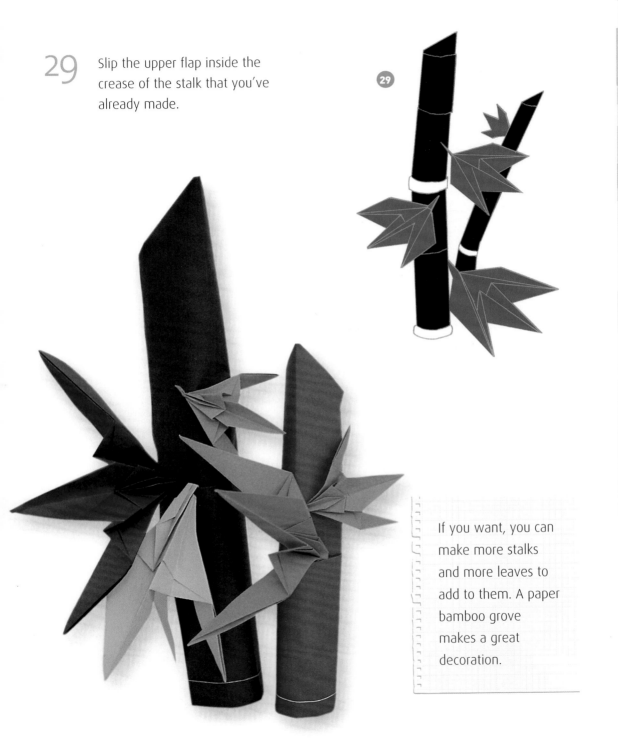

If you want, you can make more stalks and more leaves to add to them. A paper bamboo grove makes a great decoration.

TULIP

1-2 Fold along the lines to create a blintz base.

3 Fold the blintz base in half.

4 Lift each corner and make squash folds...

5 ...until you get a square. Rotate.

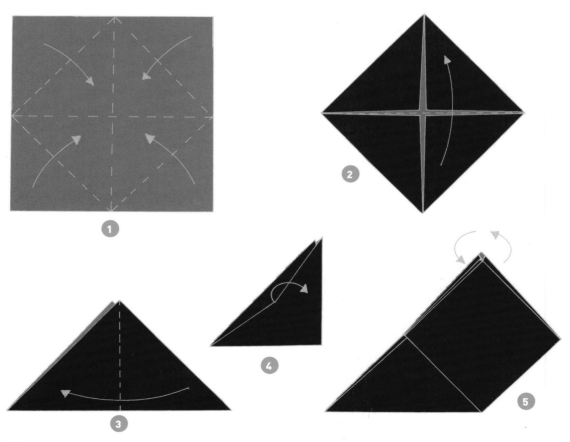

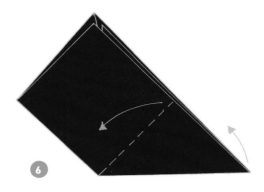

6 Repeat the last step.

7 Fold both flaps   .

8 Fold the two rear flaps backward.

9-10 Fold along the lines and repeat the same step on the other side. Spread out the corners.

11 Now you have your tulip flower.

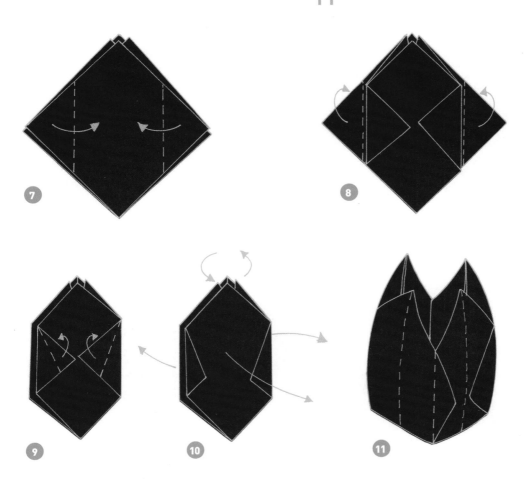

12   Fold a square piece of paper along the lines.

13-16   Fold along the lines.

17   Separate the two tips.

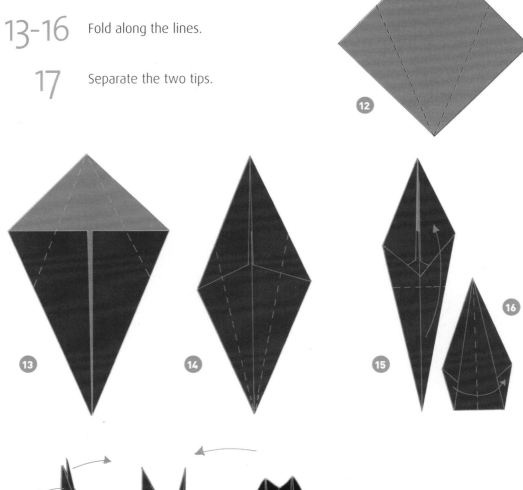

18   Make a hole in the flower head as shown in step 10, and place the tulip on the stem.

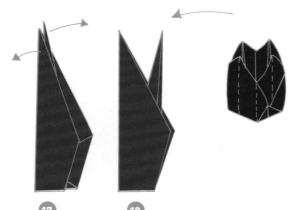

PATROL BOAT

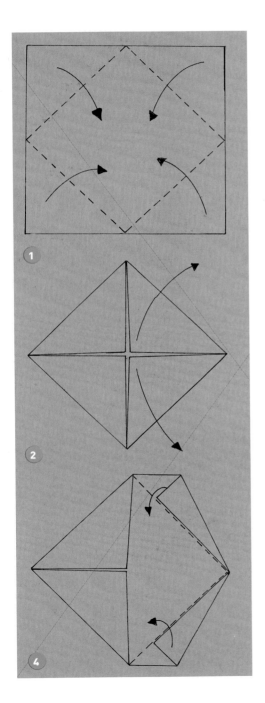

1 Fold a square piece of paper along the lines to create a blintz base.

2 Spread out two flaps on one side.

3 Fold along the lines.

4-5 Fold along the lines.

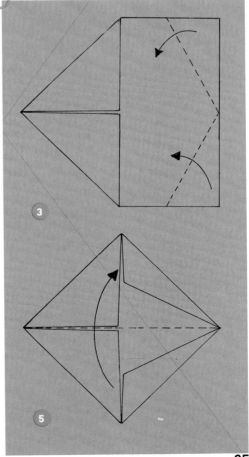

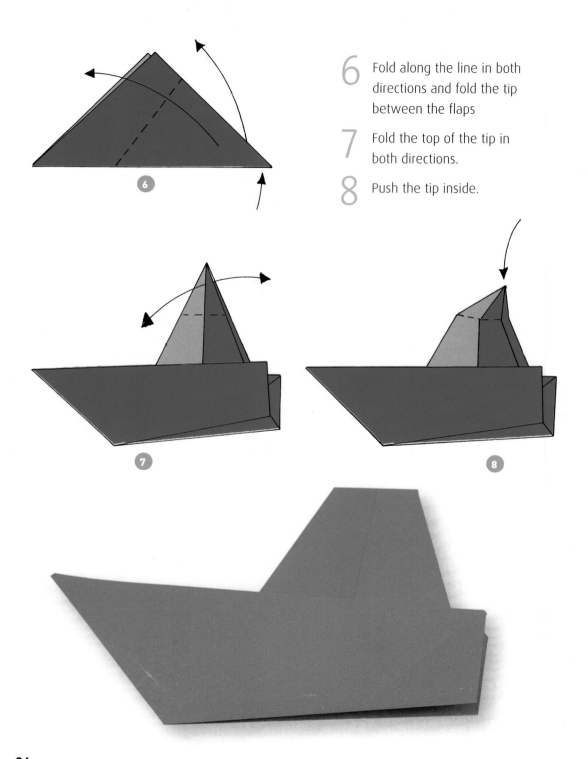

6 Fold along the line in both directions and fold the tip between the flaps

7 Fold the top of the tip in both directions.

8 Push the tip inside.

PIANO

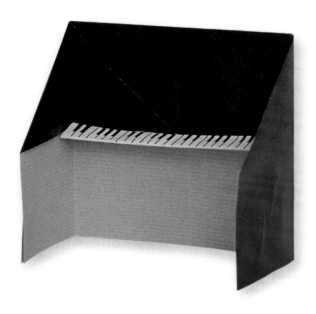

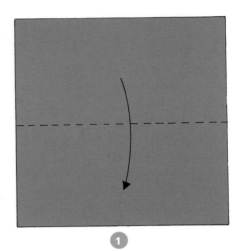

1

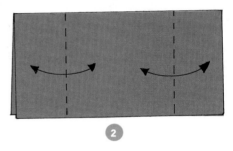

2

1-3 Fold along the lines
and spread the
paper out.

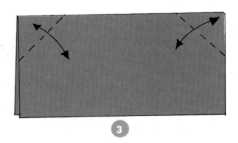

3

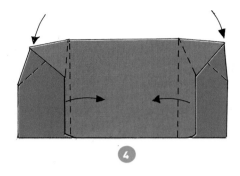

4 Lay out the corners by folding along the lines and making squash folds, like in the image.

5-7 Fold along the line.

8 Fold along the line, bringing the two flaps and the central part perpendicular to the piano.

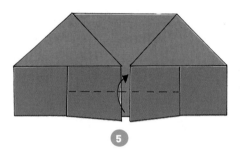

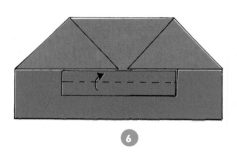

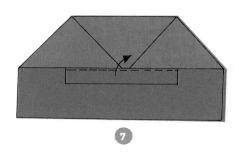

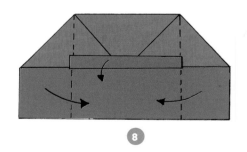

ORNAMENTAL DESIGN

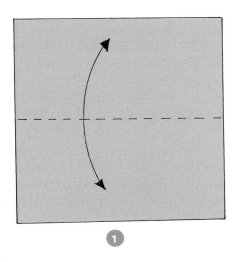

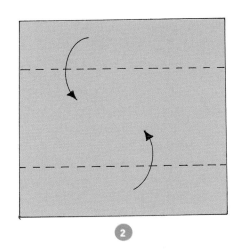

1 Fold along the line and
spread it out.

2 Fold, following the arrows.

3 Fold and spread it out.

4 Fold, following the arrows,
and spread it out again.

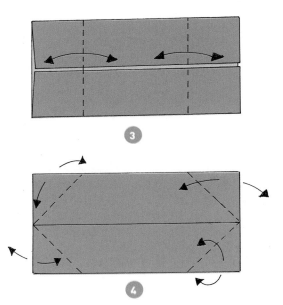

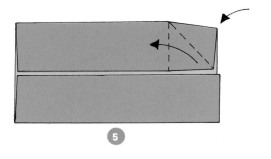

5 Lift the central part of the flap by gently pushing the tip inward.

6 Now repeat the last step with the other corners.

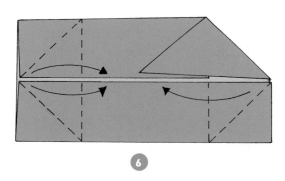

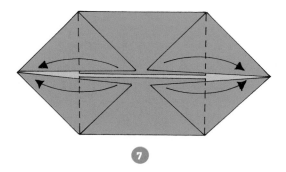

7 Fold the inner flaps to match the image.

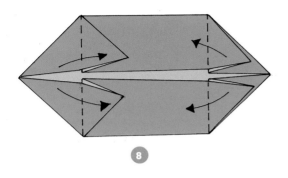

8   Unfold the inner flaps and make them perpendicular to the base of the figure.

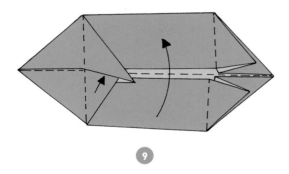

9   Slip the flaps of one side inside the flaps on the other side.

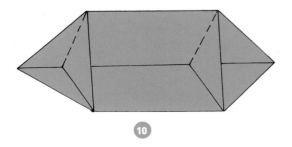

10   There you have it!

11 Build three more of
these figures and join
them to the first one.
Now you have a
beautiful decoration.
You can use glossy and
colorful paper to make
it really stand out.

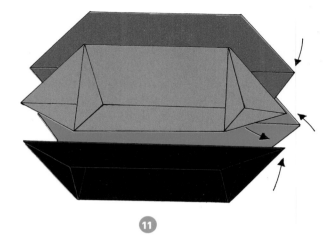

11

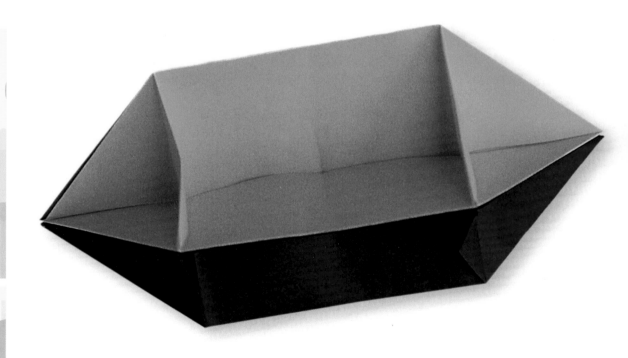

BOX

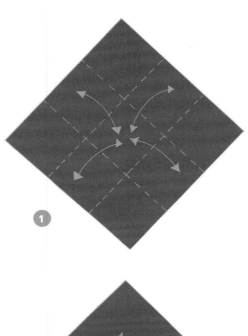

1 Create a crease pattern by folding and unfolding along the lines.

2 Fold along the horizontal axis.

3 Fold along the lines and unfold.

4 Fold until you've made the figure shown in the image.

5 Fold backward.

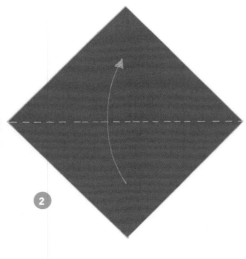

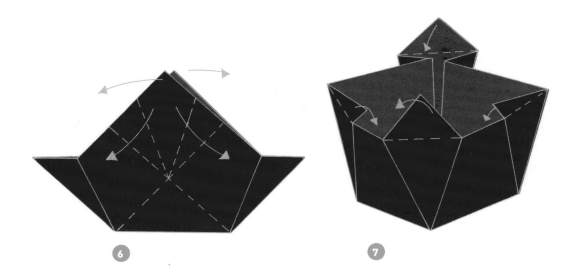

6 Spread the pattern by folding along the lines, but not too much. Pay attention to the next step.

7 Fold the flaps inward.

DECORATION

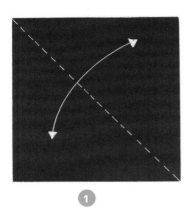

1 Fold and unfold along the diagonal line of the square.

2 Fold.

3 Turn over.

4 Fold along the line.

5 Rotate.

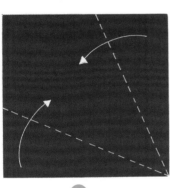

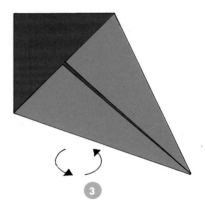

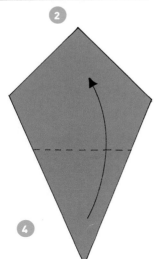

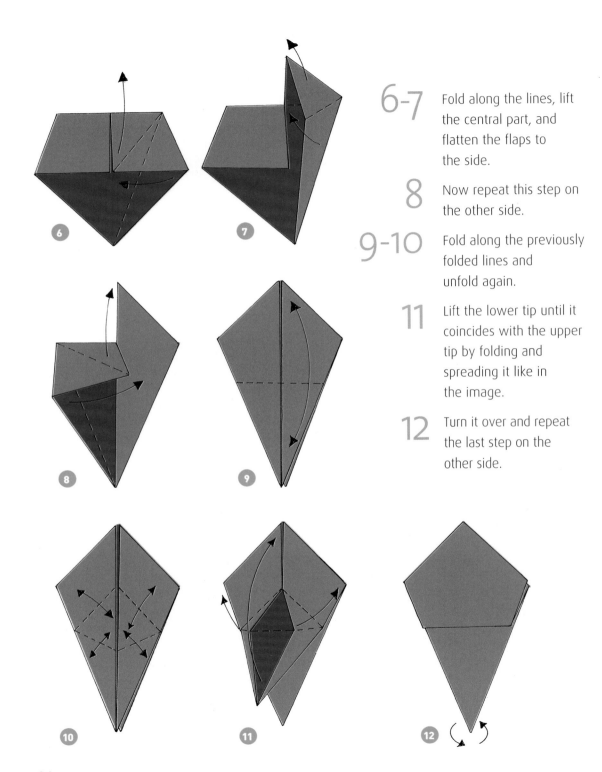

6-7 Fold along the lines, lift the central part, and flatten the flaps to the side.

8 Now repeat this step on the other side.

9-10 Fold along the previously folded lines and unfold again.

11 Lift the lower tip until it coincides with the upper tip by folding and spreading it like in the image.

12 Turn it over and repeat the last step on the other side.

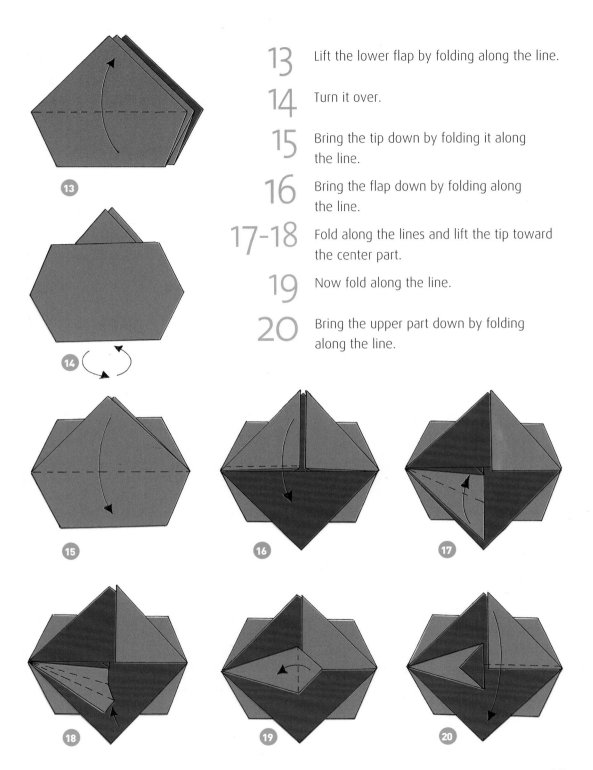

13 Lift the lower flap by folding along the line.

14 Turn it over.

15 Bring the tip down by folding it along the line.

16 Bring the flap down by folding along the line.

17-18 Fold along the lines and lift the tip toward the center part.

19 Now fold along the line.

20 Bring the upper part down by folding along the line.

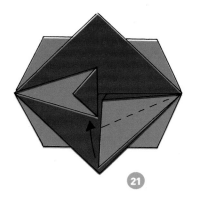

21 Fold along the
lines and bring
the tip toward the
center of
the figure.

22 Finally, fold along
the line.

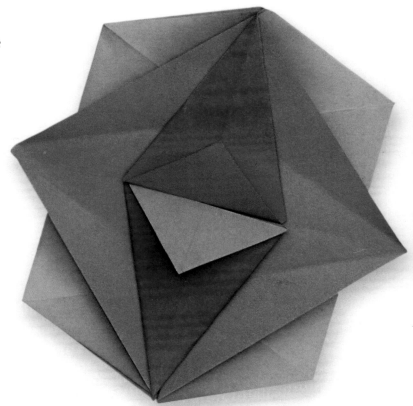

STAR

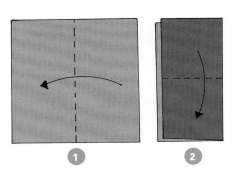

1-2   Fold along the lines.

3-4   Lift the tip and spread it out.

5-7   Repeat the same step on the other side until you have a waterbomb base.

8   Fold along the line in both directions and fold the tip inward like you see in the next image.

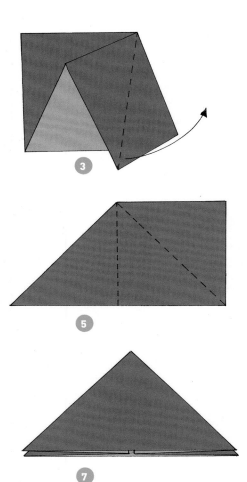

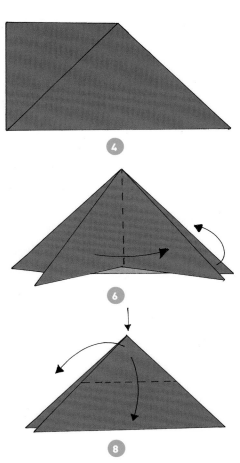

9 Fold the side tip along the line and slip it inside.

10 Repeat this step with the other tip.

11 This shape is complete. Make five more. You can use different colors if you want to make it brighter.

12 Join the four shapes together like in the image.

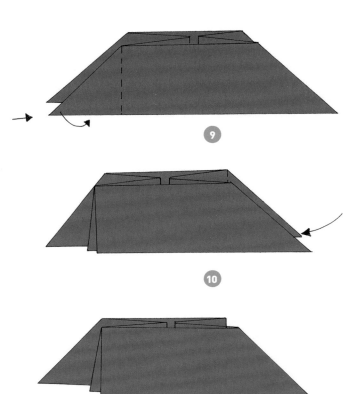

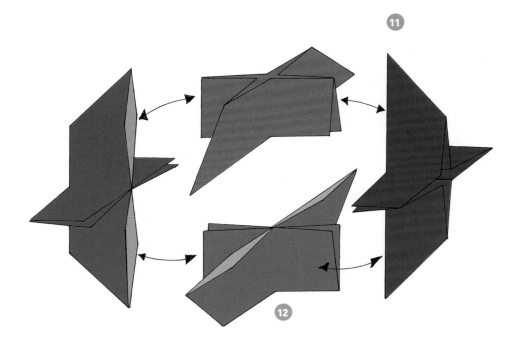

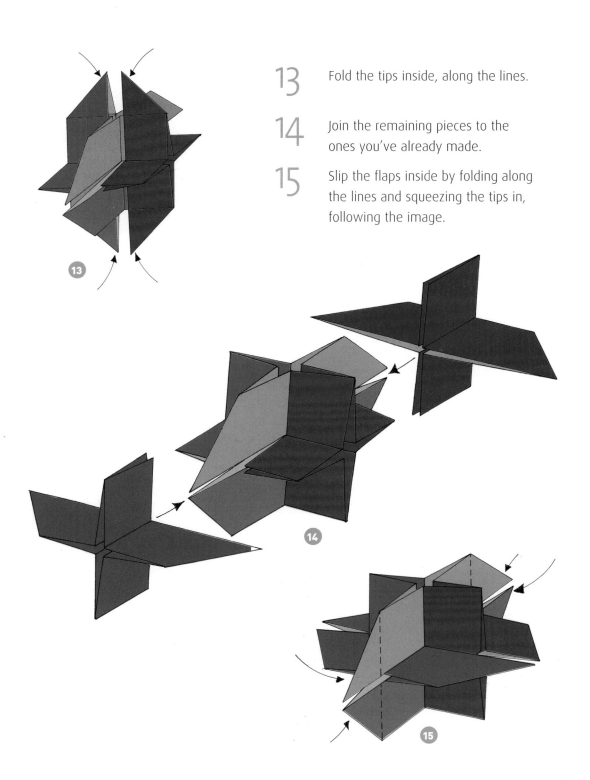

13 Fold the tips inside, along the lines.

14 Join the remaining pieces to the ones you've already made.

15 Slip the flaps inside by folding along the lines and squeezing the tips in, following the image.

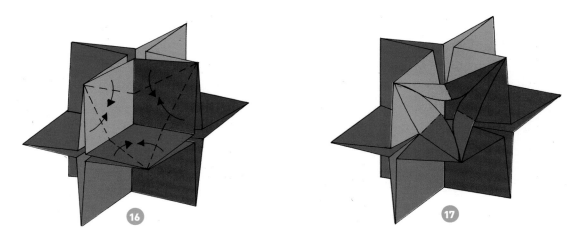

16 Fold along the lines.

17 Now repeat this step for
the remaining sides.

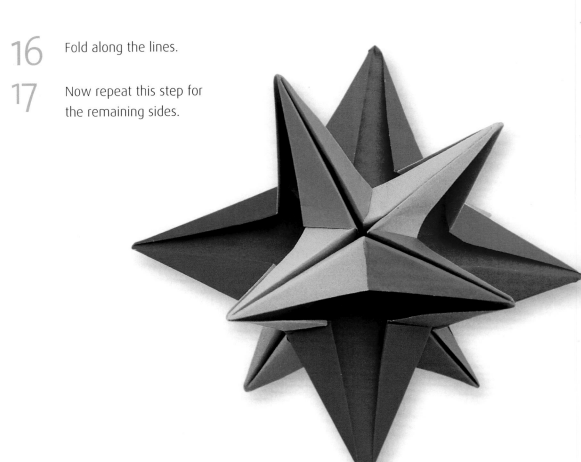

MODULAR DODECAHEDRON

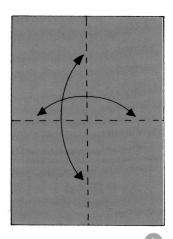

1   Fold an A4 sheet of paper along the lines and unfold.

2-3   Fold along the lines.

4   Fold along the line and slip the inner flaps together so they are connected, like in the image.

5   Bring both sides together.

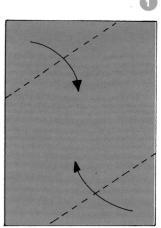

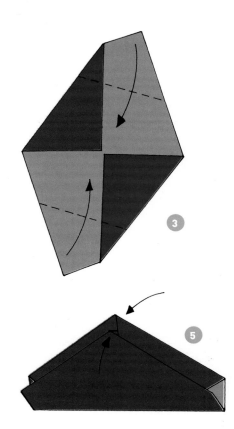

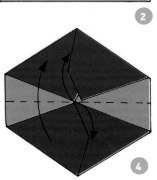

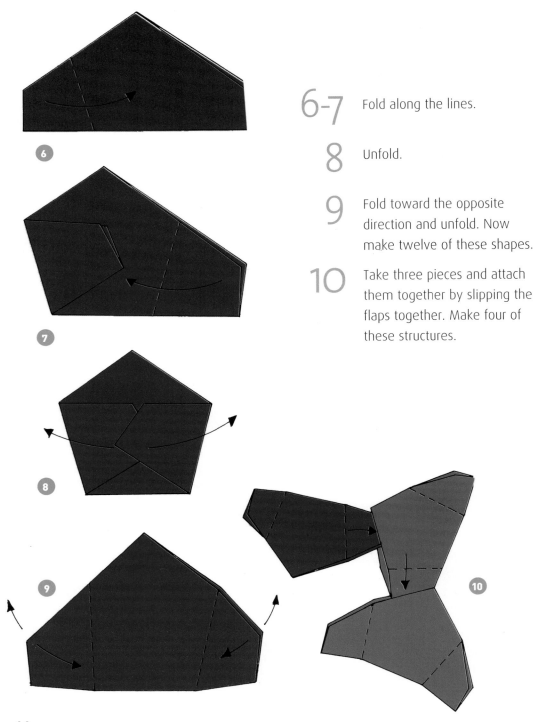

6-7 Fold along the lines.

8 Unfold.

9 Fold toward the opposite direction and unfold. Now make twelve of these shapes.

10 Take three pieces and attach them together by slipping the flaps together. Make four of these structures.

11 Attach the shapes by slipping the flaps together, like in the image.

12 Repeat the last step to join the fourth shape.

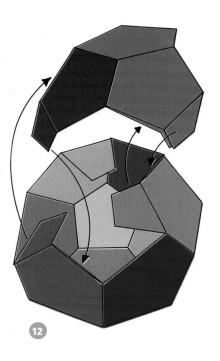

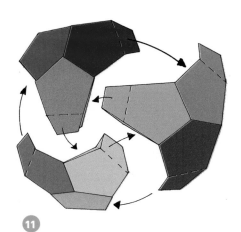

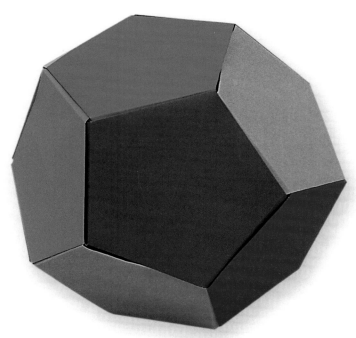

GLOSSARY

A4 sheet   A rectangular sheet of paper used in some origami designs, with the dimensions 8.3 x 11.7 inches (21.1 x 29.7 centimeters).

accordion fold   A folding technique done by creating a series of parallel creases and folding the paper over itself, mimicking the folds of an accordion.

blintz base   One of the fundamental origami bases, made by folding all four corners of the square to meet in the middle of the paper.

crease pattern   Patterns made from folding and unfolding the paper, often used as guides to create intended objects.

horizontal axis   Any line running width-wise along the paper.

squash fold   Any fold done by lifting a flap perpendicular to the paper surface, opening the flap, and spreading the flap flat to create a new surface.

vertical axis   Any line running length-wise along the paper.

waterbomb base   A fundamental origami base made by folding the paper into quarters and then squash folding each flap into a triangle, so the triangles lay on top of each other.

FURTHER READING

Books

Butler, Tom, and Michael G. LaFosse. *Origami Toys and Games*. New York, NY: Enslow Publishing, 2016.

Harbo, Christopher. *Origami Papertainment: Samurai, Owls, Ninja Stars, and More!* North Mankato, MN: Capstone Press, 2015.

Loper, Byriah. *Mind-Blowing Modular Origami: Polyhedral Paper Folding.* North Clarendon, VT: Tuttle Publishing, 2016.

Owen, Ruth. *Kids Make Origami!* New York, NY: Windmill Books, 2016.

Websites

Origami-Fun
www.origami-fun.com
Offers origami diagrams, tips, and articles suitable for all skill levels.

Origami-Instructions
www.origami-instructions.com/
Contains instructions for many types of origami, including flowers, toys, and stars.

Origami Resource Center
www.origami-resource-center.com
Provides dozens of free tutorials and introductions   into fabric folding and kirigami (paper cutting).

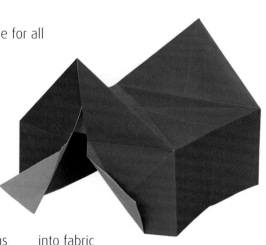

INDEX